ABOUT THIS BOOK:

The author examines mass media in light of September 11th, 2001 and asks the question-- **Is there another secret plan to attack Seattle on November 3rd?**

DEDICATION:

*To the Citizens of the Great Northwest*

Contact the Author via the Publisher at www.newworldnetwork.com

Copyright ©

## COMMENTS FROM THE AUTHOR:

- The author is NOT 100% certain Seattle Washington will be attacked, nor is there certainty on the year (2019 etc.); but the purpose of this book, is to make citizens aware of this possible threat.

- The major television networks are owned by only six corporations, is it far fetched to believe those six networks might collude to broadcast the same message, to set up in the minds of Americans the next attack?

- Media regulations should prevent vertical industry monopolies, for example; owning television, radio, books, music, film, and social media. Today no matter what the medium is, it often contains the same message.

- The mainstream media is simultaneously spoon fed global news through the press wire services, to maintain control of the narrative.

- One thing most Americans agree upon is that our elected leaders have never warned us before an attack.  Including for example Pear Harbor and September 11th, 2001.  This despite an annual defense budget that exceeds Five-Hundred-Billion-Dollars.

- Dwight D. Eisenhower if alive today would need to revise his warning to—"Beware the Military-Industrial-**Media** Complex."

# TABLE OF CONTENTS

# Introduction

*Who controls the past controls the future.*

*Who controls the present controls the past.*

**– George Orwell –**

Predictive programming is all about controlling the past.  Broadcasting and streaming images to the masses, in preparation for a future planned event.  These events may include multiple threads, paths, or a decision tree whereby a specific branch of the plan may or may not be utilized as required to deliver results.  Many might characterize this type of planning as a complex plot, covert operation, or a black operation (black op).

There is a theory circulating around the Internet, regarding the planned destruction of

Seattle Washington on November 3rd.  There is also a great deal of debate on November 3rd of which year, 2019 for example or another year.  Fearful predictions often appear and disappear, never to be seen again.  Remember the fear of Y2K in the year 2000 which never generated any significant destruction.  Unfortunately, this theory describes a potential atom bomb or high energy beam, creating an event worse than 911 if that is even possible.  For this reason, a closer examination of this Seattle attack theory is important.

Looking back in time prior to 911; the evidence is overwhelming that advance knowledge of the event by many people is much more fact than fiction.  Researchers discovered thousands of 911 clues hidden in films, magazines, books, cartoons; and other forms of mass media.  Some of these media clues are simply too obvious to pass off as coincidence or conspiracy theory. There seems to be credibility in the notion that vast powers are at work behind the scenes to plan, implement, and deploy coordinated "predictive programming" against the population through multiple mass media platforms.

If there is a secret plan is to attack Seattle, why would plotters put these hidden images in the mass media and expose their own plan. One line of thought is if you are warned and ignore the signs, in some twisted way they cannot be blamed for murder if the victims are cooperating. Another idea is that they want you to find the hidden images and by placing these images in the public consciousness their eventual narrative will be accepted. This seems to be the most plausible, a form of mass brain-washing.

Such mass manipulation of our entire country would encompass lots of agents and media companies.  These media corporations would have to be infiltrated at the highest levels with American traitors.  There would have to be secret orders, secret codes, and secret communications providing a way for these agents to coordinate their evil actions.  Keeping all these agents in line would require payment or blackmail.  Continuing this line of thought you begin to say—it is impossible, due to the magnitude of the operation.  However, consider the following.  A university study concluded that China with a population of 1.3 Billion is controlled by only 7 people.  There is no doubt that the USA could be under the control and manipulation by only a handful of people at the top.

# Chapter 1: Identifying the Clues

Perhaps the origin of the Seattle November 3rd theory, can be tracked down to the magazine cover published in 2015 by the Economist. Certainly, it is true that the Economist is owned by wealthy dynasty families including:  Agnelli, Cadbury, Rothschild, Schroders, and Layton.  The group is almost entirely based out of the United Kingdom.  With such vast wealth, perhaps bored their only joy is to mess with (kill) other people and achieve world conquest.  Such was the dream of: Marx, Hitler, Mao, and Ceil Rhodes for example.  Each psychopath simply wanted their unique version of their twisted new world order.

Another dubious organization when it comes to the field of mass mind manipulation is called the Tavistock Institute, also based in the United Kingdom.  The Economist magazine headquarters is only three miles from this institute.  The President Trump Russian Collusion dossier came from the United Kingdom's MI6 agent Christopher Steele.  Has the table been set for an attack on Seattle blamed on Russia, to jump start world war III?

When the Economist magazine was published in 2015, there were many news reports about this ominous magazine cover.  It was not solely conspiracy theorists who were pointing this out.  For example, the Vigilant Citizen published an article—"The Economist 2015 Cover is Filled With Cryptic Symbols and Dire Predictions."  They were not alone, many journalists had questions about this dark and creepy magazine cover.

The wealthy elitist owners of the Economist magazine are also connected to the secretive cabal known as the Bilderberg's.  The 2014 Bilderberg meeting took place in Denmark June of

2014 and the magazine was published on January 2015.  Is it conceivable they finalized their plans at this meeting and then printed their magazine cover to initiate the operation?  This seems to be a most plausible explanation given the timeline. Going back further in time to examine the mass media, evidence of clues being embedded goes back as far as 1963. So even if the operation did not get the green light until 2015, it was conceptualized much early; along with other potential targets around the US.

Examining the 2015 Economist cover to find many clues.  Here is the list of the primary clues which indicate a pending attack on Seattle Washington, on Sunday November 3rd.

**PRIMARY CLUES:**

1. FOOTBALL

2. GREEN TURTLE

3. JET FIGHTER

4. TWO YELLOW FLAGS

5. OBAMA

6. MISSLE

7. NUCLEAR EXPLOSION


Why would the elite warn the masses of he attack before it happens, giving away their evil plans?  There really is no need to understand the disturbed mind of murdering psychopaths intent on harming women and children.  Pure evil simply exists; this was sufficiently demonstrated on September 11th, 2001.  Maybe the cabal sleeps better at night knowing they warned everyone; and since no action to stop them was taken they are somehow forgiven of their sins, good luck with that twisted rationalization.

In addition to the primary clues, you will these secondary clues.  They are noteworthy to examine and will be further explained in the next chapter.

**SECONDARY CLUES:**

8. HELICOPTER

9. PANDA BEAR

10. BATTERY

11. CHILD EATING

12. FLUTE PLAYER

What follows is the 2015 Economist magazine image for study; review the image to locate the primary and secondary clues.

The Economist
ヒラリー・クリントン「女性の雇用」　メアリー・バーラ「車がしゃべる」
デビッド・ブレイン「マジックの未来」　ビル・ゲイツ「子供たちを救う」
ミシェル・バチェレ「全員の政治」　カール・アイカーン「行動する株主」
日経BPムック
日本語翻訳権独占
日経BP社
2015
世界はこうなる
The World in 2015

# Chapter 2:  Each Clue Explained


It is important to look at each clue in light of the basic hypothesis, an attack upon Seattle Washington.   How does each clue relate to such an attack?


THE PRIMARY CLUES ON THE ECONOMIST MAGAZINE COVER:


**CLUE 1:  FOOTBALL** – The football clue is often displayed along side a baseball, especially in cartoons.  When you see both together football-and-baseball it points toward Seattle Washington where the NFL football stadium is located right next to the MLB baseball stadium.

**CLUE 2:  GREEN TURTLE** – The turtle is slow but methodical.   Green in color it may represent Seattle, the city is known as the green "emerald city" similar to that described in the "Wizard of Oz."  Some researches have pointed out that the turtle is also the symbol of Fabian Socialists, see photo below.  Karl Marx wrote that Socialism was the bridge to Communism, which seems to be the chosen system for the United Nations world

government.  Like the turtle "drip-by-drip" the

Fabian Socialists slowly marching to take-over

America and the entire world.

**CLUE 3:  JET FIGHTER** – There are plenty of

jets in film and on television; this of itself is not

alarming.  However, having a jet on the Economist

cover might be important.  Since there is only one

jet and not a squadron, the implication is that this

one single jet will deliver a large bomb to Seattle.

**CLUE 4:  TWO YELLOW FLAGS** – The first yellow flag shows "11-5" and the second flag shows "11-3."  Having the flags bright yellow, indicates that the two series of numbers are very important to the plan.   These numbers will be discussed in depth in a later chapter.

**CLUE 5:  OBAMA** – Former President Hussein Obama is featured prominently front and center on the magazine cover.  Does this indicate Obama is a key planner for the attack on Seattle?  Recalling that Obama was also the 44th president; this clue most likely is pointing to the number 44.  Below is a 2017 Poster for Seattle's Key Arena, the artist JayZ knew the significance of 44.

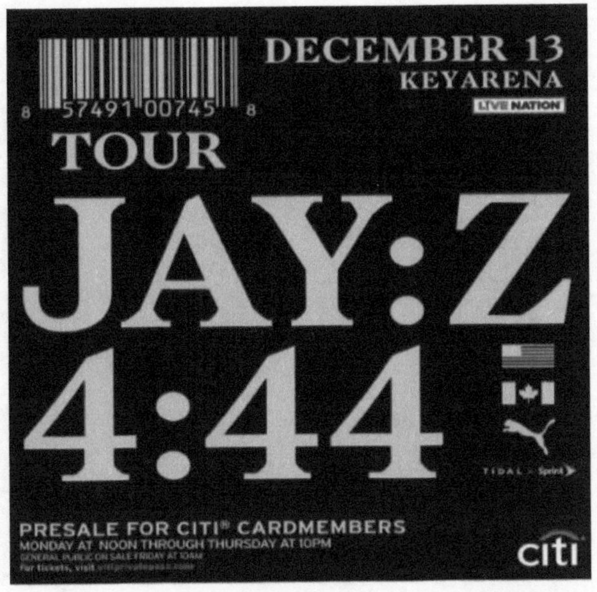


Below is a scene from the JayZ concert, real nice burning the eyes out of American citizens when the attack on Seattle takes place.

**CLUE 6:  MISSILE** – This type of missile resembles an intercontinental ballistic missile. Repeated quite often in the news, is how North Korea has been testing intercontinental ballistic missiles.   However, the fact that the missile is launching upwards could be misdirection.  For example, it conflicts with the jet fighter which would drop a bomb downward.

**CLUE 7:  NUCLEAR EXPLOSION** – This clue is next to the missile, clearly pointing to a nuclear attack on Seattle.  It supports the previous clue of an intercontinental ballistic missile.  It is rather obvious this is the narrative they want the public to accept.  It is their projection when the true type of attack may be different, is it possible to fake an incoming missile?

SECONDARY CLUES ON THE ECONOMIST MAGAZINE COVER:

**CLUE 8:  HELICOPTER** - There are too many movies and films with helicopters to make much from this clue, but why post it on the cover?  Most likely this is a tip off for the citizen's of Seattle.  If you are attending an event and see helicopters, there may be a very limited time to exit the location.

**CLUE 9: PANDA BEAR** – This clue is pretty obvious, it is pointing to China.  Will this attack be blamed on China is one question.  Perhaps it means once the initial attack is launched, China may attack also.  It may indicate after Seattle is attacked, Chins grows significantly as a global power.

**CLUE 10: BATTERY** – This clue indicates that one aspect of the attack on Seattle may be a power outage.   However there is a scenario where the power is turned off in California, to power the weapon pointed at Seattle.

**CLUE 11: CHILD EATING** – This child is actually eating instant noodles mixed with hot water.  The message is clear, during a prolonged power outage there will be food rationing.  If you are in the Seattle area, prepare accordingly.


**CLUE 12: FLUTE PLAYER** – Most likely the flute player is a reference to Krishna the Hindu God. The word comes from the Sanskrit word Krsna, which means the darkening; this is likely another reference to a power outage.  There is a different Hindu God "Shiva the destroyer" statue outside CERN headquarters in Geneva Switzerland (666 Logo below) and it is possible that CERN is a global weapon system disguised as a research institute.

Examining the media images in Chapter 4, reveals that the Economist clues are often bundled with other objects.  Even if these exact objects are not on the Economist magazine cover; it supports the theory that there are multiple paths in attack planning that may be carried out against Seattle.  Some of the bundled clues commonly appear along with the magazine clues:

-   SEATTLE SPACE NEEDLE

- SEATTLE FERRIS WHEEL

- SEATTLE SEAHAWKS STADIUM

- GOODYEAR BLIMP OR HOT AIR BALOON

- SUBMARINE


These additional objects may indeed be part of the overall plot.  For example, the space needle, Ferris wheel, and Seahawk stadium could be bomb targets.  The blimp and submarine could be a method to deliver a bomb, although the magazine cover had the fighter jet.  There are just so many images of these objects exploding in the media samples to pass off as coincidences.

Many believe the 11-3 theory is only a psychological operation to instill fear on our population.  That may very well be, but on the other hand; this is a very labor-intensive effort to go to this much trouble across all forms of media such as film, cartoons, television, magazines, album covers, etc.  More likely this is indeed a plot to destroy America as 911 was a prior step.  Ultimately this is an attack on freedom and the free enterprise system of America.

# Chapter 3:  The Attack Weapons

Before examining the predictive programming evidence, consider different types of weapons which could be deployed.  An attack may contain one or more of these elements, here is a brief description of each weapon system.

- **Real Nuclear Attack**

- **Fake Nuclear Attack (Made to look like a Nuclear Attack)**

- **Weather Weapon (Tsunami, Hurricane, and Wildfires)**

- **EMP Weapon (Power Outage)**

- **Conventional Bomb (Blimp, Building, Space Needle)**

**REAL NUCLEAR ATTACK** – A real nuclear bomb will destroy a 1 to 2 mile radius from the blast point; then will disperse radioactive dust for 10 to 20 miles depending upon the wind.  This would be a bomb size of 15 Kilotons consistent with what was used at Hiroshima in 1945.  Today there are Megaton size bombs which would make these blasts significantly larger; but to smuggle into Seattle a larger size weapon adds more risk. The Hiroshima bomb was ten feet in length and 2 feet in diameter.  Do the elite really want their mansions in Seattle uninhabitable for quite a few years?  There are also many scientists who believe the entire existence of a working nuclear bomb is an elaborate hoax that has been maintained to keep the war machine humming.  Those in this camp believe that much of the damage at Hiroshima Japan was done by carpet bombing to create the appearance of nuclear devastation.

**FAKE NUCLEAR ATTACK** – This is an interesting concept, the idea of the elite causing mass panic by faking a nuclear bomb attack.  How might one go about creating this illusion?  The technique of carpet bombing as claimed in

Hiroshima, would be much harder to pull off in Seattle with everyone walking around with a cell phone video camera.   Another way to pull off this fake attack is to first drop a conventional weapon, one which would generate the same mushroom looking cloud as a nuclear bomb.  The most obvious choice would be what is known as a fuel-air explosive or FAE, which is a Thermobaric weapon that relies on atmospheric oxygen as fuel. This is possible because there are many cartoons such as the Simpsons featuring of all things Oxygen in a cartoon.

The common FAE weapon often in the news is the MOAB or Mother-Of-All-Bombs, which really means Massive Ordnance Air Blast.  This type of bomb will make a mushroom looking cloud very similar to a nuclear bomb.  There is only one big problem.  The blast radius would only be 150 to 300 meters; versus the  2000 meter plus radius of a nuclear bomb.  This radius would be way too small unless you had a secret trick.  A method to drop the MOAB and simultaneously use a different type of weapon to incinerate a larger

radius to make it appear like a nuclear bomb, go

to the next weapon.  Pictured below is a MOAB

and beneath that the MOAB mushroom cloud.

**THE WEATHER WEAPONS** – Now there are different types of weather weapons none of which can be confirmed because they are top secret. But many government insiders have said they exist and congress has held hearings on weather weapons.  So lets for now assume they exist. Perhaps there is a way to create a Tsunami, direct a Hurricane, or create an Earthquake.  A natural disaster in Seattle would be tragic, but would not generate public support for a world war.

However, what if the elite have a secret weapon, a Directed Energy Weapon (DEW) that was tested in California.  Could this type of weapon be used to <u>expand the blast radius</u> of the conventional MOAB to simulate a nuclear bomb blast radius of 2000 plus meters?  This seems to be the trick they might use against the citizens of Seattle next, lets explain further.

What appears to have been used in California is a two part system.  The first part seems to be electromagnetic targeting system, it is set to a particular material frequency like steel. The steel would be used in home construction (nails) and in automobiles, but trees would not contain steel.  After thousands of targets are lit up, pulsating laser bursts are sent to hit each target.  The laser bursts are invisible; to those on the ground it appears that homes and cars are spontaneously combusting into ash.  This describes exactly what was seen in the wildfires of California, homes and automobiles burnt to ash, but trees are still standing just fine.  This kind of weapon system might be satellite or aircraft based, however it is also possible it is operated on the ground and here is why.  When officials claim they are turning off the power to California homes to limit wildfires from spreading; could they

actually be diverting power to the weapon
system?

The homes and cars are completely burnt,
the trees are fine.  As the twin towers on 911
turned to dust, could it be possible this weapon
system was also used on September 11th, 2001.  In
fact, the California wildfires left puddles of molten

aluminum from automobile rims; similar to the puddle of melted steel from the twin towers. Intensive heat that was able to melt metals.  The California wildfires incinerated neighborhoods in a very similar appearance to Hiroshima.  This would be the objective to create the mushroom cloud with the MOAB and then expand the destruction radius to create a FAKE NUCLEAR Attack on Seattle.

For the theatre of a fake nuclear attack there may be homes incinerated as shown in the California fires image below.  There will be claims America was attacked by a nuclear bomb.  The area would be closed off by the military, and some limited radioactive material may even be exposed for the few scientists they allow into the area with their Geiger counters to measure radiation levels. The American people will again be duped into going to war.

**EMP WEAPON**– An Electromagnetic Pulse (EMP) Bomb is typically exploded in the air and designed to take out the power grid.  Seattle could be plunged into a prolonged period of darkness.  On March 29th, 2019 President Trump signed an executive order directing federal agencies to protect the USA from an EMP attack.  However, unless the outage cascades to the entire nation; not sure it would generate the launching of a world war.  An EMP weapon does not have mass casualties until society degrades in time, making this type of attack is unlikely.  A nuclear attack (or fake nuclear attack) may also take out the power grid.

**CONVENTIONAL BOMB** - Traditional explosives could be placed in a building, in the Seattle Space Needle, in the Blimp flown into the stadium.  However the attack would be too small to launch a war.  There is nothing of the size and prestige of New York's Twin Towers.  This type of attack is unlikely, except for as a distraction or bundled with the nuclear or fake nuclear attack.

The Goodyear blimp is an interesting attack possibility, for example there is a film from 1977 about an attack on a football stadium with a Goodyear blimp.  At the website

**www.Goodyearblimp.com** there are three blimps-- Wingfoot 1, 2, and 3.  The call sign for Wingfoot 3 is of all things, N3, as in November 3$^{rd}$ perhaps.  The schedule says that on November 3$^{rd}$ Wingfoot 2 is suppose to be in Miami Florida.   It does not say where Wingfoot 3 is, could it show up in Seattle?

When discussing an attack on Seattle much of the media predictive programming may point to Seattle; but this could be misdirection and the real attack occurs on the West Coast but in a different city.

The discussion of a real nuclear attack or a fake nuclear attack has many considerations, technical challenges, and long term impacts.  If a mushroom cloud rises in Seattle, Uranium-235 for example used in Hiroshima has a half-life of 704 million years.  How was it that 2-4 weeks after the bomb hit Hiroshima most of the radiation was gone and people could return to the city?  History records that the plans to build the Hiroshima bomb were destroyed, very convenient.  This discussion really calls into question the entire concept that nuclear weapons even work; making the odds of a FAKE nuclear attack in Seattle much more likely.

With this background in the types of weapons that might be deployed against Seattle, it is time in the next chapter to start looking at the predictive programming evidence pointing to a Seattle attack on November 3rd, 2019.

# Chapter 4:  Predictive Programming Evidence

These media images demonstrate that indicate an attack upon Seattle Washington on November 3rd is plausible.  In displaying these images the author adds news commentary on media images under The Fair Use Doctrine.

The Simpson's cartoon series held hundreds of clues pointing to September 11th, 2001.  The creator Matt Groening has been identified is a high level Freemason and his name appeared in Jeffrey Epstein's personal phone book.  Before looking at Seattle images, lets examine a few regarding 911.

**FIG 1 The Simpsons** – Bart Simpson in 1997 displays a nine-dollar magazine with the New York Twin towers behind it, providing the code 911.

This would be fourteen years before the actual event.  The word "coupon" in the lower right corner is what many believe stands for- coup on, takeover of the US government.

**FIG 2 DC Comics** – This cover was released in 1985, the 911 is rather obvious and note the word "Chaos" toward the bottom.  It is difficult to know if the artists are aware of what they are doing or they are just completing an assignment from upper management.  With 911 investigations still moving forward, it would be good to see

these artist's interrogated; there is no statute of

limitation for accessory to murder.

The previous two examples were simply to demonstrate how going back in time there is clearly 911 predictive programming.  This time around if an attack on Seattle is being planned,, the public can get ahead of the game.

**FIG 3 The Simpsons** – For an attack on Seattle Washington, the date of November 3$^{rd}$ is clearly seen as 113.  There has been mention that many cartoon artists refer to 113 as a first year classroom at California Institute of the Arts; this seems to be a convenient cover story, since many artists did not even attend this school.  The "A" in this photo most likely is code for atom bomb, once you discover other Simpson images clearly display the atom bomb.

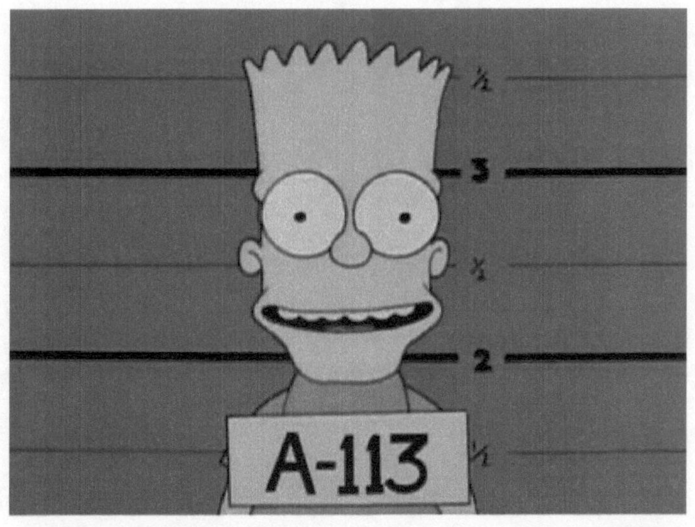



**FIG 4 Unknown Cartoon** – Here again is the A113, indicating Atom Bomb on 113 or November 3rd.

**FIG 5 The Simpsons** - Homer displays the devil horns sign along with the reversed 113 revealed as 311.  This number 311 appears often in other films such as War Games.  Homer wearing a black t-shirt may point to the film Black Sunday.

**FIG 6 Simpsons DC Comic** – A reference to the Devil is often featured in cartoons such as this Simpson's Comic Book as Bart holds the Devil pitch fork known as the "trident" and note that a giant trident was incorporated into the rebuilding of the World Trade Center.  Notice issue number #19 is this a reference to the year 2019?

**FIG 7 The Simpsons**– Moving now into the football stadium attack scenario, this image shows the football stadium, also notice the "Duff Beer Blimp" which is often displayed in Simpson cartoons.  The simple and sick code could simply

be "Snuff" as in killing thousands of football fans, snuffing out their lives.

**FIG 8 The Simpsons** – In the same episode of the Simpson's with the blimp and football stadium, a flash of missiles launching can be seen in this image.

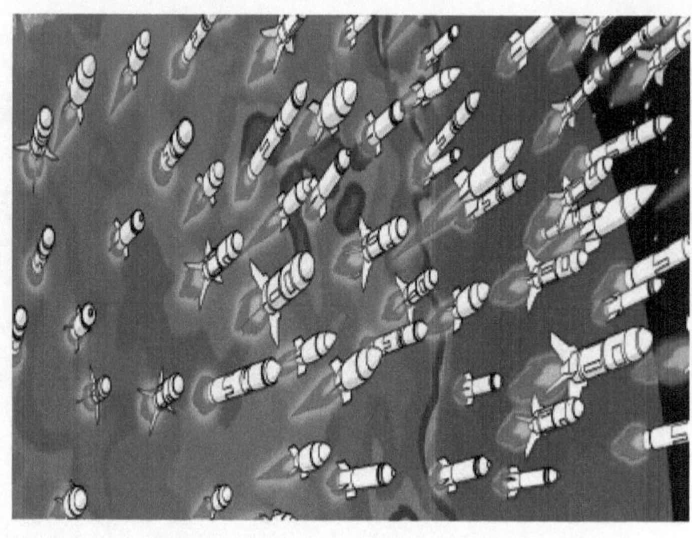

**FIG 9 The Simpsons** – Demonstrates "panic"
as the football stadium crowd runs from some
kind dripping substance resembling cartoon fire.
One interesting thing to know is the open sky
similar to the Seattle Seahawks stadium with the a
very similar lattice steel structure for a closing the
roof in bad weather.  The Seattle stadium is very
unique, this similarity is way beyond coincidence.

**FIG 10 The Simpsons** – Zoom in on the

robot in the crowd to see that this cartoon artist

has sick sense of humor offering "grief

counseling" to the victims.  This artist certainly

deserves to be arrested if this vision comes true.

Look closely and you will the girl holding the

devil's pitch fork, a very strange item to take to a

football game.

**FIG 11 Film Black Sunday** – This film was released in 1977 featuring a terrorist attack on a football stadium.  The crowd panic's when the Goodyear blimp descends upon the stadium carrying a bomb.  The letters OWL are on the blimp, most likely the plan was to attack the Super BOWL, but then changed to a "regular game."  In one episode of the Simpson's Homer asks his boss for-- Super Bowl Tickets, then Playoff Tickets, then Regular Game Tickets.

**FIG 12 Film Black Sunday** – This image shows Goodyear blimp coming into the stadium where it is about to strike the light stand.

**FIG 13 Film Black Sunday** – As the blimp comes into the stadium there is sheer "panic." This image shows the crowd where behind the woman is the word BOM as in bomb.

**FIG 14 Film Black Sunday** – A bus transporting fans to the stadium displays the number 4403, this supports President Obama the 44th president and the 03 portion of the bus number refers of course to November 3rd.

**FIG 15 Calendar** – At this point it is important to recognize the significance of the number 44.  There are 52 weeks in a year and November 3rd ends the 44th week of the year 2019, see Wk below.  Practitioners of Satanism (and Human sacrifice) use weeks; a year i.e. 52 weeks = 13 x 4, their favorite number is 13.

## November 2019

| Wk | Mo | Tu | We | Th | Fr | Sa | Su |
|----|----|----|----|----|----|----|----|
| 44 |    |    |    |    | 1  | 2  | ③ |
| 45 | 4  | 5  | 6  | 7  | 8  | 9  | 10 |
| 46 | 11 | 12 | 13 | 14 | 15 | 16 | 17 |
| 47 | 18 | 19 | 20 | 21 | 22 | 23 | 24 |
| 48 | 25 | 26 | 27 | 28 | 29 | 30 |    |

**FIG 16 Film Batman** – This film Batman The Dark Knight Rises, was released in 2002 and features an attack on a football stadium by a villain.  This image displays the damage that the bomb blast caused to the field.

**FIG 17 Film Batman** – This is the kickoff for the game, the blast occurs just after the game kickoff.  The interesting thing to note is that the kicker is number 19 which again may indicate this operation is being kicked-off in 2019.

**FIG 18 Film Batman** – The villain in this movie is pictured here as "bane" it is an odd spelling because you would think it would be spelled "bain."  When you run numerology gematria on "bane" you will find both 13 and 322. Input the big letters UPMC in this photo you get 19 mostly likely meaning 2019.  This is using the website www.gematrianator.com.

**FIG 19 Film Batman** – The crowd in this image seems normal, but one-and-only-one male spectator has their hand inside their jacket like Napoleon or Albert Pike, the Hidden Hand pose of the Freemasons.   All this data pointing toward the Occult, Satanism, and Freemasonry indicate that those in these secret societies know all about this planned attack on America.

**FIG 20 Film Batman** – A close up of the stadium press box, note the number 322 which connect to Yale University's Skull and Bones Secret Society.  This will be a very important connection specifically to the Seattle Seahawks Stadium.

**FIG 21 SEATTLE SEAHAWKS STADIUM MAP**

– The seat map of Century Link Field in Seattle. Do you see the section that is missing, there is no section 322, but there is 321 and 323.  Currently there is no evidence that the Seahawk owner Paul is a member of the Skull and Bones Society, but Mr. Allen passed away in 2018, so maybe he knew too much.

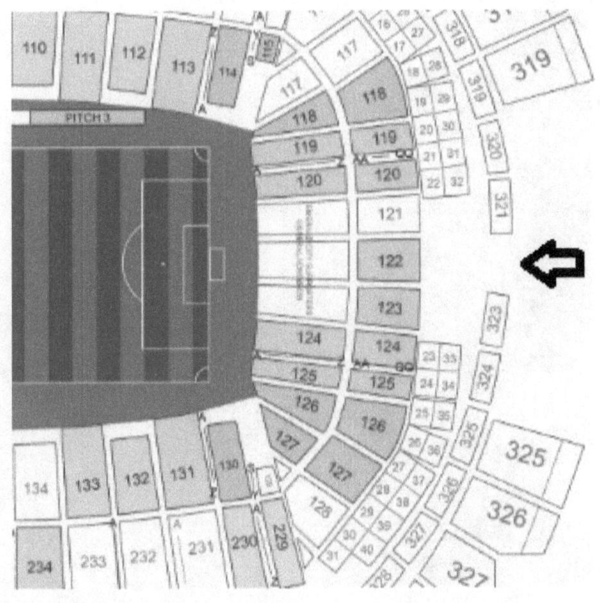

**FIG 22 BATMAN FILM**– This image shows the eerie similarity between the batman film uniform LEFT and the real Seattle Seahawks uniform RIGHT.  It appears the artist essentially inversed the colors.

**FIG 23 SEATTLE SEAHAWKS GAME ON NOVEMBER 3$^{RD}$** – In 2019 this just happens to be a Sunday as in "Black Sunday" perhaps.  From the esoteric standpoint this is most likely driven by those that worship the Black Sun.  Below is the image of the Seattle Seahawks opponent on November 3$^{rd}$, the Tampa Bay Buccaneers; side-by-side with the 322 emblems of Yale's Skull and

Bones Society.  Give all of this information, would you and your family attend this football game?

**FIG 24 LED ZEPPELIN** – Remember in the film Black Sunday the blimp carrying a bomb lands in the football stadium; consider this image published in 1973 from the rock band Led Zeppelin.  Zeppelin is another word for a blimp, just a coincidence?  This certainly looks like a

MOAB bomb hitting a stadium crowd, it does not even look like a blimp.

**FIG 25 LED ZEPPELIN** – Here is another image of a different Led Zeppelin album, can you find the 11-3 hidden in the image?

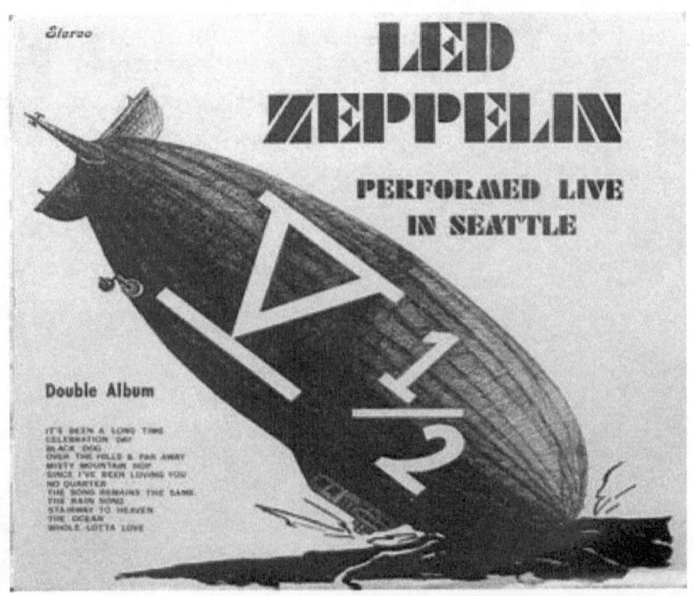


**FIG 26 LED ZEPPELIN** – In case you can't find the 11-3 the number 11 is highlighted in red and 1 + 2 = 3, this generates the required 11-3 date.

After removing the 11, the remaining letter "V" is very symbolic in the occult and the Nazi's wore a letter "V" on their sleeve, it does not stand for victory it stands for Vulcan.  The Nazi party originated from the Thule Society in Germany and the American Chapter of the Thule Society is known as Skull and Bones.  This connects to the Seattle Seahawks whose owner Paul Allen has an investment company he conveniently named Vulcan Inc. don't be fooled by his Star Trek cover story.  Vulcan means the Roman fire God aka the Devil.

**FIG 27 BATMAN FILM**– This is a still shot of an explosion that forms the famous bat wings. Maybe it is an ink blot test but when you turn it upside down, it looks like it could be the Seattle Space Needle exploding, you be the judge.  Recall there are different attack scenarios with the stadium being just one scenario and the Space Needle a different scenario.

**FIG 28 THE SIMPSONS** – This image is another episode showing the football stadium, but there are hints to the atom bomb.  The hidden messaging is so obvious; the real operation may actually be a FAKE Atom bomb.

**FIG 29 THE SIMPSONS** – This image is another reference to the atom bomb but should the dumbed down masses not get it, the artist has a guy in a bright red shirt wearing a nuclear mushroom cloud hat, how blatant can they get?

**FIG 30 WAR GAMES** – This film came out in 1983, the famous line from the computer was- "Do You Want to Play a Game" and Matthew Broderick types in "Global Thermonuclear War." The computer then asks which side do you want to be.  Interesting how the Trump Administration and Russian Collusion has taken form since 2016. Will the attack on Seattle be blamed on Russia?

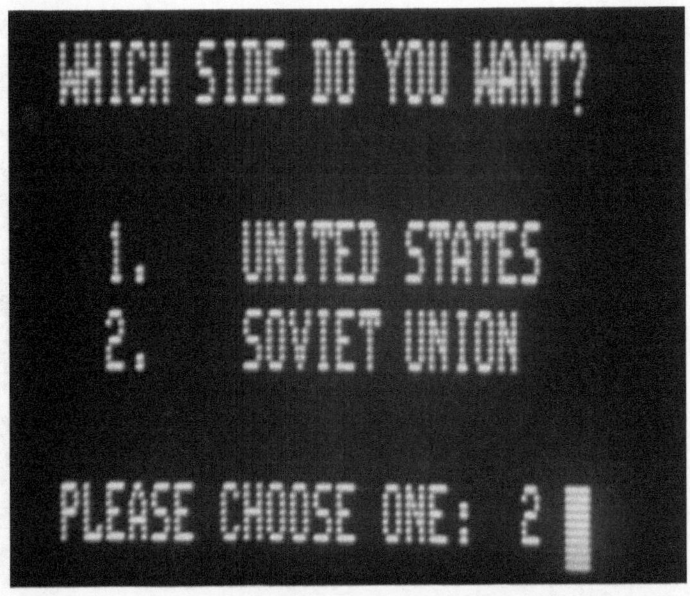


**FIG 31 WAR GAMES** – Next the computer asks Matthew Broderick to enter the targets and look what he inputs.  It appears Las Vegas already suffered a different type of attack, but the attack in Seattle may be much bigger.

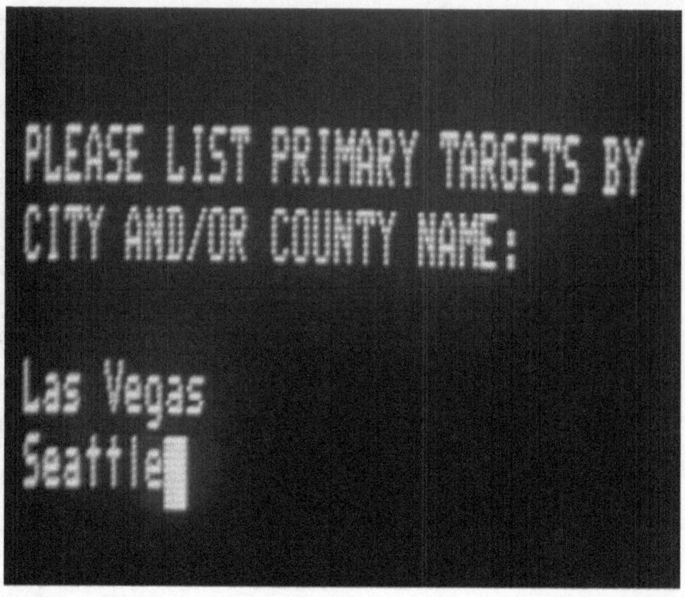



**FIG 32 WAR GAMES** – This image from the film shows phone number area codes in the computer system, note the fictious area code 311 which is the inverse of 113.  The 311 code first appeared in 1963 in a television show called Route 66. Was this the earliest date of planning for the Seattle Attack?

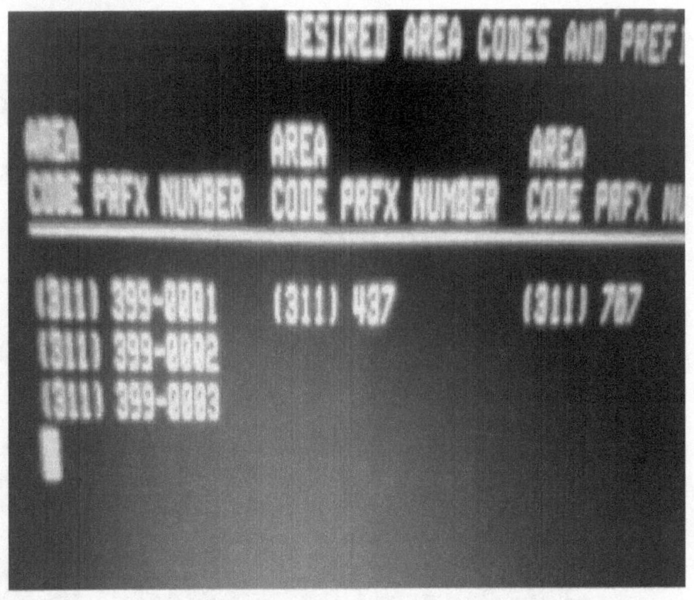


**FIG 33 MATTHEW BRODERICK** – This image from the 1986 film Ferris Bueller's Day Off.  There are 3 actors and above them is number 22, together forms the code number 322 yet again.  They may symbolize three attacks on America as the red jersey number is number 9 for 911.  Why messaging was placed into this film versus other films may have to do with the name Ferris as in Ferris Wheel.  The hat that Ferris wears with the

yellow box represents the US 32$^{nd}$ Cavalry

Regiment; but minus the emblem it resembles a

Nazi or Russian Submarine cap, and cartoons such

as the Simpsons feature lots of submarines.

**FIG 34 CALL OF DUTY** – Even video games

have predictive programming.  In this image of

"Call of Duty World War Three" released in 19XX;

the same 113 code appears.  See green

highlighting to part of the Letter W below, even

more shocking is that this video game was released on November 3, 2017.  Was the actual plan to elect Hillary Clinton in 2016 and launch World War III in 2017?

**FIG 35 CHAOS** – The film "Chaos" was released in 2005, in the film a close-up of the actor's wrist watch reveals the code 113.

**FIG 36 ZOMBIELAND** – The first of a series of films was released in 2009, below in the picture in the lower left is most likely the Seattle Ferris Wheel, which would not be built until 2012. There have been many large Zombie festivals in Seattle, what fun dressing up as future nuclear attack victims. Since the film was not centered around an amusement park or county fair, placing

the Ferris Wheel on the film's cover can only be to
send a subliminal message.

**FIG 37 ZOMBIELAND** – The Zombieland
Black SUV with the hidden November date, added
pink highlight to reveal the 113.  Isn't interesting

out of so many numbers the car is number 3; and
out of so many colors the car happens to be black
(as in Black Sunday).

**FIG 38 ZOMBIELAND** – A different car from
Zombieland a Black Limousine with the hidden
113, added yellow highlight to reveal the 113.
This is not any regular black limousine, this is the
President of America's Limousine; does this mean
the President is dead and now a zombie?

**FIG 39 ZOMBIELAND** – Just in case you missed the death of the President, here is an image of the deserted Whitehouse, symbolizing the death of the American Free Enterprise System (Capitalism).  This image seems to be similar to Ferris Bueller's **FIG 33**, in that three people standing in front of the deserted Whitehouse symbolize three attacks on America including 911 and Seattle.

**FIG 40 SIMPSONS** – Going back to the Simpsons cartoon show, this image does not show a blimp but it does have a balloon (almost a blimp) and it connects to atomic power, flying over the nuclear plant.

**FIG 41 SIMPSONS** –  This same balloon in this same episode flies over the Notre Dame Cathedral which caught on fire April 15th, 2019.  It appears that this is a signal to launch the attack on Seattle in 2019.

**FIG 42 SIMPSONS** – There are many mentions of Seattle in different episodes of the Simpsons, but this image has both the iconic Space Needle and the number 113.  This one they are being really tricky, but the two hairs on Homer's head form the 11 and the single hair by his ear is the number 3.   Let your imagination soar like a blimp or a plane that drops a bomb.

Also note that the Space Needle is lit up like a high energy beam is hitting it.

**FIG 43 MARS ATTACKS** – In this image the Space Needle is indeed hit with a high energy beam weapon from a Mars invasion space ship. Don't let them fool you with trips to Mars and Aliens, the high energy beam is a man made weapon behind used on Americans, as was done in the California wild fires.

**FIG 44 SEATTLE SUPERSTORM** – This film was released in 2012 and it shoes the intent of destroying the Space Needle just like many other forms of media.  This Seattle attack may occur in multiple locations simultaneously.  Do not be up in the Space Needle on November 3rd.  Also take note of the helicopter in this image, another connection to the Economist magazine cover.  The storm is so powerful it destroys buildings but the

helicopter is out flying about?  Also note three lightening bolts is this another reference to three attacks upon America or will the high energy weapon hit three targets or display three bolts? The elite have a sense of humor, they even named their WNBA team the Seattle Storm.

**FIG 44 PEARL JAM** – A Seattle rock band formed in 1990.  A Seattle poster, not sure the year but it shows the bombs falling and a very large perhaps nuclear explosion in the top left.

**FIG 45 TAYLOR SWIFT** – You would think that this clean innocent young artist would be

pretty tame, but look at her Seattle Tour.  The devilish serpent weaves through downtown Seattle, she knows exactly what is planned.

**FIG 46 ITCHY AND SCRATCHY** – This animated television series is part of the Simpsons related Krusty the Clown show.  Oh its real funny watching their fellow Americans citizens burned to death with a high energy weapon.

**FIG 47 SEATTLE FIREFIGHTERS** – This television series launched on March 22$^{nd}$ 2018, and it is actually called Station 19.  Gee, wonder why they picked number 19 could it be a signal to attack Seattle on 2019?

**FIG 48 WORLD ORDER** – This synchronized robotic dance video was released in 2018 as a claimed mocking President Trump music video. They filmed in Seattle of all places and are standing in front of a big number 13 (McDonalds). In this image they hold up the number 1, see next image.

**FIG 49 WORLD ORDER** –  In this image they hold up the number 3.  So when you view their entire music video, it flashes 1 and 3, pointing to 113?

**FIG 50 WORLD ORDER** – Another had sign
they flash is this kind of open hand downward,
this is the "boom sign" as in bomb blast.

**FIG 51 THE QUEEN**– Here is the Queen and Prince Harry reading a brochure, go to next image.

**FIG 52 THE QUEEN–** Harry is pointing at one runner.  The Jersey number reads 239 (2+9 = 11 and the 3 gives 113), go to next image.

**FIG 53 THE QUEEN–** Harry gives the same creepy hand gesture as the World Order Music Group, in the audio Harry actually says "boom." These elitists all know what is coming for Seattle.

**FIG 54 PRESIDENT TRUMP** – Trump gives the number 1 sign.

**FIG 55 PRESIDENT TRUMP** – Trump gives the number 3 sign, in this case it also forms 3 sixes or 666; in actual video you will see Trump flash 1 and 3 often.

**FIG 56 LOCAL SEATTLE MEDIA** – A local news station runs a special about the state of Seattle, just a coincidence or subliminal messaging?  Remember even the local stations are owned by the six media conglomerates.

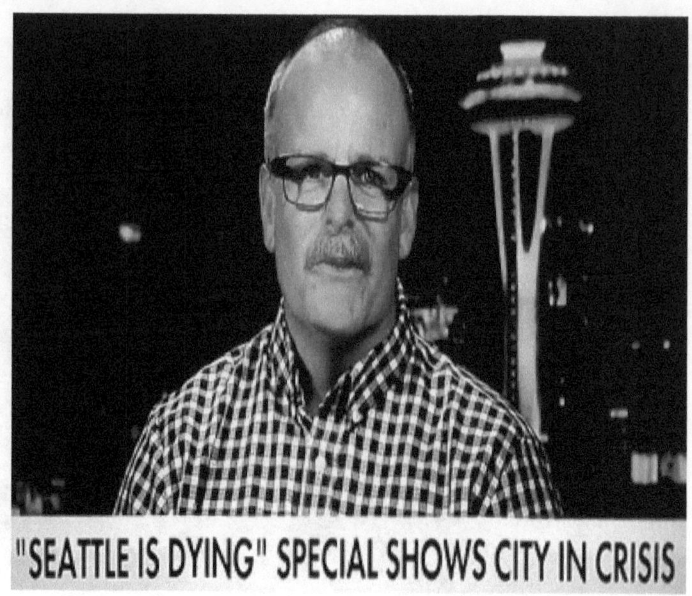



**FIG 57 PAUL ALLEN** – Owner of the Seattle Seahawks football team.  He receives the ring of honor? Is this really for football or for destroying Seattle and killing his friends?  Look at the date and you will see the code, 113.

**FIG 58 VULCAN INC** – Previously covered was the letter "V" and word "Vulcan" but here is a video capture image from Vulcan's website showing a missile hitting the baseball stadium that resides next to the football stadium?

**FIG 59 SIMPSONS** – Most likely the most important clue of the entire attack operation is the green turtle, Homer gives good advice in this image.

**FIG60 SIMPSONS** – Very odd Bart Simpson is sitting on a turtle in this image.  If you Google "Simpsons Turtle" you will find plenty of instances of turtles in Simpson episodes.

**FIG 61 SEAHAWKS STADIUM** – Can you see the turtle in the seating chart?  The owner Paul Allen was directly involved in the design details of the stadium.  Was it Mr. Allen himself who created a Turtle hidden in the seat map?  There will be a special place in hell for Mr. Allen, if Seattle is attacked in a lake of fire.

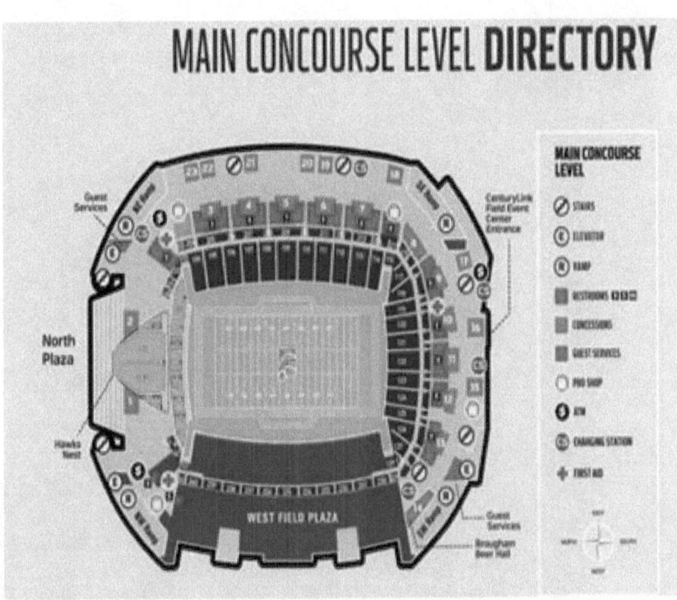


**FIG 62 TERMINATOR** – In Terminator 2: Judgment Day, during a flashback a nuclear bomb explodes with this chilling image.  Is this what the elite want to do to the citizens of Seattle with their high-powered energy beam.

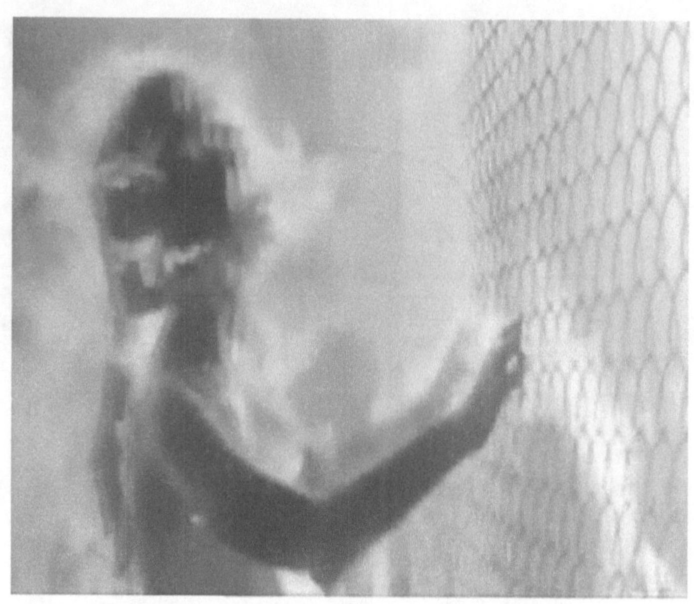

**FIG 63 TERMINATOR** – Intense flames but the GREEN TURTLE does not burn?  Exactly what happened with the California wildfires with a Directed Energy Weapon. Houses incinerated but the trees next to the houses were not burnt.

**In totality the evidence is overwhelming**.

There is a clear pattern, a common thread from cartoons, to film, to video games, to music.  The elite in power have been planning this attack on Seattle for some time, and have embedded subliminal predictive programming into the media.  Keep in mind this fifty image sampling only scratches the surface of hundreds to thousands of images.  The reader should expand their mind and conduct their own research; but certainly should not be in Seattle on November 3rd.

Films and television also have audio; whereas this manual is limited to visual images. For example, when the real Hindenburg crashed in 1937, the newspaper headlines repeated what an eye witness said—"Oh the Humanity."  When you watch cartoons for example, besides connecting November 3rd to Seattle, they often use the same Hindenburg words.  In another example a television news anchor talking about North Korea, mentions that Seattle might be hit by North Korean missiles.  General Michael Hayden a former director of the CIA stated that by the end of the Trump Presidency, North Korea will be able to reach Seattle with a nuke.  Relative to this book, there is a great deal of audio that goes along with the theory.

What is presented in these images is only the tip of the iceberg.  Watching the above listed films and television shows might generate hundreds of additional clues.  How many more media sources, films, and television shows exist with more embedded predictive programming. There is more than enough evidence for a court of law.

# Chapter 5:  The Date of the Attack

It is not for sure an the attack will take place in 2019.  Maybe the attack was planned for an earlier year and has been canceled.   On the other hand, evidence such as the number 44 per **FIG 15**; clearly points to the year 2019.

The first thing that is obvious from the 2015 Economist magazine cover, are the numbers contained in Clue-4-Two Flags.   The first set of numbers are "11-5" and the second set of numbers are "11-3."   To most people the simple explanation is that an attack will occur on November 5th or November 3rd.  The reason most researchers are suggesting November 3rd, is that most mass media predictive programming displays the numbers "113" more than "115." Some people point out that November 3rd in

European format would be "311." Here again "113" is seen in the mass media much more than "311" or "511."

There are additional and significant observations that point further to a November 3rd attack in the year 2019 versus other years.  First off, November 3$^{rd}$ is indeed a Sunday in year 2019; see **FIG 11** regarding the movie "Black Sunday." Furthermore, on this Sunday in 2019, the Seattle Seahawks do have a football game against the Tampa Bay Buccaneers and the connection to the Skull and Bones Society per **FIG 23**.

Another idea is to take the numbers on the magazine cover 11-5 and 11-3 and note that 11-4 is missing; maybe November 4th is the attack date?  Adding the numbers together 3 + 5 = 8 and maybe November 8$^{th}$ is the date?  With all the numbers added up, 1 + 1 +5 + 1 + 1 + 3 = 12 and maybe the attack date is the 12$^{th}$.  If the ones are elevens, the math changes to 11 + 5 + 11 + 3 = 30, generating an attack date of the 30th.  So although it seems simple with the two flags on the magazine cover; there could still be many different combinations.  They are giving us hints; but they do not want to be caught or stopped.

The bright yellow flags certainly appear to be the key, the flags are very bright yellow, they want us to look at those numbers.  The flags are yellow perhaps a 2nd meaning is yellow cake uranium.  Why would yellow be used with Seattle is the green emerald city?

Many readers may have heard about QAnon, the anonymous poster whose riddles first appeared on the 8chan public bulletin board.  QAnon has posted about three booms; could this mean three bombing targets in Seattle?  QAnon has often stated "watch the water" could this be regarding a submarine off the west coast?  On

November 3rd of 2017, QAnon post 68 talks about HUMA as most assume is Huma Abedin; but the last sentence of this post says- "Alice and Wonderland." On the 2015 Economist Magazine is Alice and Wonderland.

There is much debate about the exact attack date; but sometimes the most obvious answer is the best; and the majority of the evidence points to November 3rd, there is some evidence for 2019 but nowhere near the amount pointing toward November 3rd or 113. Unfortunately everyone will have to wait and see what happens in Seattle every November 3rd.

# Chapter 6:  Location of the Attack

There is a good amount of predictive programming point toward Seattle, but this could be misdirection for an attack that is launched on a different city.  There has been activity in California with wildfires and power outages; maybe this is the real target on November 3rd?  On January 13th, 2018 a ballistic missile alert was issued in the state of Hawaii.  Do you see the hidden message January 13th is again 113.  It was later claimed that this alert was in error; but could it have been a test for the alert that will be issued in Seattle on November 3rd?  One thing for sure, it is the west coast that is seeing plenty of activity.  On October 17th, 2019 FEMA led "The Great Washington ShakeOut" to be prepared for a big earthquake; or was it really preparation for something else?

Most evidence indicates attack will occur in Seattle Washington with multiple possible scenarios.  The bombing or flying a blimp into the football stadium located at Seattle's Century Link Field.  Fighter jets that may attack Seattle by air. An intercontinental ballistic missile possibly launched from a submarine.

Will all three of these attacks take place, one after another or at the same time?  Do these scenarios simply represent evil option A, B, or C; and until a final decision is made as to which option will be deployed against Seattle? Are all these scenarios misdirection; for a different attack scenario.  Are these embedded clues simply part of an on-going threat to keep the public living in a state of fear?

Considering the sequence of events that could take place in Seattle; the evidence points to first a large bomb which is perhaps followed by an air attack.  In the case of North Korea they have over 800 combat aircraft and 300 helicopters.  If the Pear Harbor like attack is carried out by North Korea then most likely there are rouge elements running North Korea or they are taking order from a larger power like China.  No nation would launch such an unprovoked first strike against America without expecting to be destroyed.  There are many films and cartoons that display squadrons of attacking enemy aircraft.  For example, the 1984 film about a US invasion called "Red Dawn."

There is always the possibility that once the initial attack occurs on Seattle, the larger nations such as Russia or China will launch a secondary attack.  Perhaps these larger nations are being manipulated to start World War III.  It is possible that the motive is economic; which country will own the primary digital currency.  There are also movements of gold bullion behind the scenes; and perhaps gold bullion payments are not being met. There was no aircraft attack after September 11th, but that was confined to buildings; not an entire US city.

In 2019 there has been increased talk of United Nations troops being positioned inside the US borders.  There has been talk of stealth troops being smuggled into the US under the guise of immigration at our Southern Border. These sleep cell troops could be waiting for something big to take place before they make their appearance. There have been many UN treaties signed (by US politicians) but are still waiting for ratification (approval) by our democratically elected congress and senate.  This may not be possible; unless the US is attacked and citizens disarmed.  America will not stand by while our nation is placed under UN-Foreign rule; yet this seems to be the plan. The location of the attack may be centered in downtown Seattle; but the attack may expand to the entire USA.

# Chapter 7: Patsies and Motives

Considering the many reasons why they might be targeting Seattle for destruction.  The proximity of Washington State to North Korea or Russia would immediately come to mind.  Although the state of Alaska is even closer to these nations; Alaska has rich oil reserves.  The targeting of Washington State ahead of Alaska; leads to the conclusion that a real nuclear bomb may still be on the table (despite the fake nuclear attack idea).  If a real nuclear attack was launched against Alaska, those oil reserves could not be tapped for many years due to fallout contamination, hence why Seattle was selected.

Once President Trump was elected in 2016, the Russian collusion narrative began; blaming a Seattle attack on Russia is in line with the mass media promotion of the Russian collusion.  There was an incident with a Russian submarine catching fire on July 2nd, 2019 off the west coast.  Recall the Ferris Buehler hat **FIG 33** and the Beatles album in 1968 "Yellow Submarine" could it be describing Yellow Cake Uranium?  What about the Uranium One deal with the Russian owned Rosatom in 2010?  Has the official narrative already been set that Russia launched a nuclear missile from a submarine off the west coast?

November 3rd holds political significance as the founding day of the Socialist Republican Union (USR) versus 311 or March 11th for example.  If the goal is truly to create a global socialist government this could be the reason 113 was selected.  This is also the day when Skull and Bones 322 got their first member elected president to begin the take-over of America, traitor William Howard Taft in 1913.

When a crime is committed there is no requirement to prove motive, but there are a few possible goals.  First, is Freemason Albert Pike whose dream predicted three world wars would be required to bring about a new world order. What is this new world order all about, this will be the subject of a separate book but for all practical purposes it is a world dictatorship disguised as eco-socialism.  An attack on Seattle may be designed to start World War III between Judaism and Islam; then promise world peace under a new world government system (that makes all traditional religions illegal).

With America being a largely Christian (Judaism) nation; blaming the attack on radical Islamic terrorism seems plausible; perhaps originating out of Syria or of Iran.  If you examine the list of wars you would also discover a pattern of the USA attacking (in self-defense of course) right down the line a list of countries with the most oil reserves.  The next country after Iraq is Iran, this attack on Seattle might generate public support for sending troops into Iran and ultimately a take control over of Iran's natural oil reserves by oil corporations (owned by the elite).

It shouldn't be underestimated the Economist magazine clue of the panda bear. Recently Trump administration policies include a trade war against China and including removing China from control over Los Angeles ports.  Does this set the narrative that the attack on Seattle may be blamed on China?

The most probably patsies are—Russia, Syria, Iran, North Korea, or China.  The big bonanza for military spending however; is the lucrative Bush Doctrine 911 scam—to blame the incident on an undefined Radical Islamic Terrorists and any country that supports them, an open check book to attack any nation.

# Summary

*The very word "secrecy" is repugnant in a free and open society; and we are as a people inherently and historically opposed to secret societies . . ."*
**– John F. Kennedy –**

Thank you to the many researchers who have exposed this theory as an honest effort to warn the people of Seattle.  This book has attempted to consolidate a wealth of research into one concise manuscript adding new viewpoints and opinions to the debate.  Based on 911 this new threat is credible enough to write about.  The plot was probably conceptualized in the early 1960's.  In 2015 when the Economist magazine cover was published, the plot was most likely activated and code named "green turtle."

Faced with the over-whelming evidence in the media image examples of mass media predictive programming; any open-minded citizen will agree that something dangerous is in the works.  The reader is encouraged to examine additional media and search for more clues, signs, and symbols.

It is discouraging, the number of large media companies—CEO's, directors, and perhaps artists that are involved in creating this programming.  It must be an immense and very evil industry; an even wider cabal pulling the strings to inject all of this programming into the American subconscious.  If an attack on Seattle does occur, it will be interesting to see if the wealthy elite such as Microsoft's Bill Gates and Amazon's Jeff Bezos are suspiciously absent that day from the state.

If an attack upon Seattle occurs, there must be a call for the arrest of the board of directors of the Economist as a good starting point; including their parent holding company EVOR NV based in the Netherlands.  They may not be running the operation, but they would be worthy of arrest and interrogation; to determine who sits at the top of the sinister pyramid.

Unlike September 11th, 2001 today there is more ability see and understand the hidden symbols; which may be their downfall.  There is no place in a peaceful society for secret clubs with legalized discrimination; and permitting secretive organizations to operate in the shadows without public and press transparency.  The elite at the top may by providing orders, but these secretive organizations including rogue intelligence groups are performing the operational tasks on the ground.  These secretive organizations are the hand tools utilized to carry out evil plots against humanity; these are war crimes plain and simple.

The new world order which these attacks seeks to create, will backfire into a world that ends secrecy.  The new world most needed is one where mankind will no longer sacrifice fellow citizens to achieve political goals of world conquest.  The evils of war, false flags, and sacrifice are unsustainable against the power of truth and freedom.  Citizens of the world have an innate ability to see truth and justice; regardless how much propaganda and programming is deployed.  Efforts of tyrants throughout history have failed and will fail again.

To those that live in Seattle, please take this theory into consideration as you go about your daily life; to do the wise thing to protect yourself and your loved ones from this threat.  The author hopes that the plot against Seattle will not be carried out or will fail.  That these potential attack dates come and go without incident; and American citizens remain safe and secure.

*Was the Seattle Seahawks "Legion of Boom" promotion just a cool advertising campaign or a planned assault by the wealthy elite upon the citizens of Seattle?*

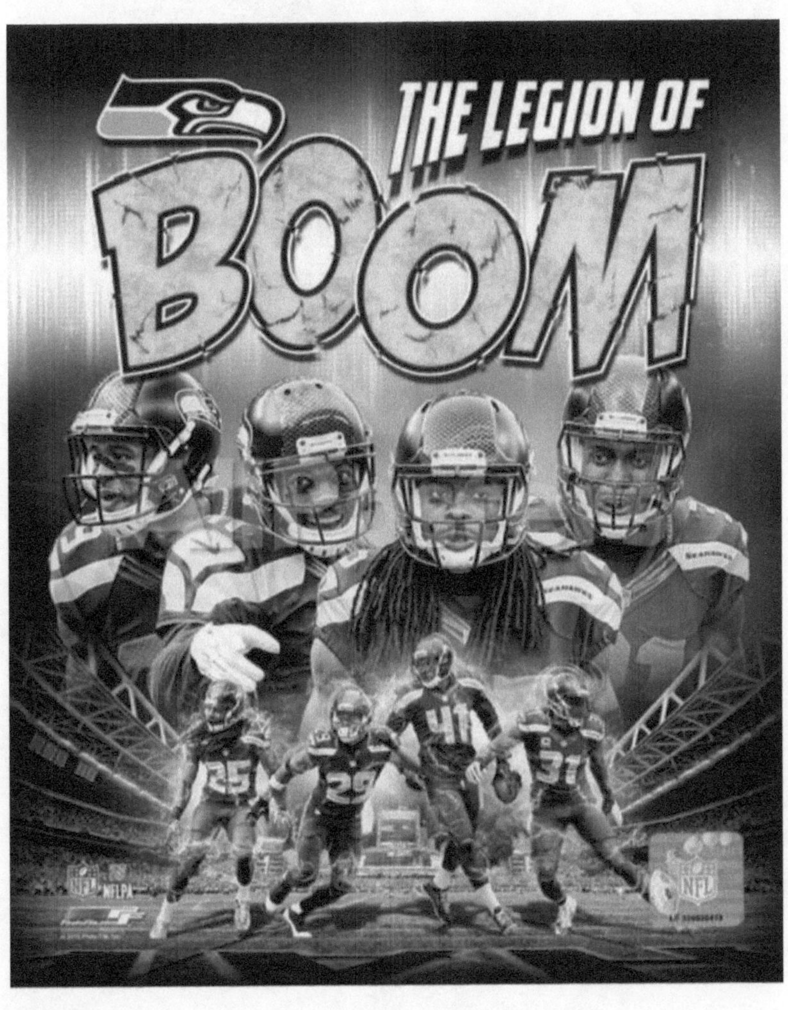

*Unfinished Business to build a One World Government, no cap on the pyramid.*

*What takes place at a pyramid? Sun Worship Temple? Human Sacrifice?*